Date: 11/30/11

The Inuit

KEVIN CUNNINGHAM
AND PETER BENOIT

Children's Press®
An Imprint of Scholastic Inc.
New York   Toronto   London   Auckland   Sydney
Mexico City   New Delhi   Hong Kong
Danbury, Connecticut

Content Consultant
Scott Manning Stevens, PhD
Director, McNickle Center
Newberry Library
Chicago, IL

Library of Congress Cataloging-in-Publication Data

Cunningham, Kevin, 1966–
  The Inuit/Kevin Cunningham and Peter Benoit.
    p. cm.—(A true book)
  Includes bibliographical references and index.
  ISBN-13: 978-0-531-20760-4 (lib. bdg.)   978-0-531-29302-7 (pbk.)
  ISBN-10: 0-531-20760-9 (lib. bdg.)   0-531-29302-5 (pbk.)
  1. Inuit—Juvenile literature. 2. Eskimos—Juvenile literature. I. Benoit, Peter, 1955– II. Title.
  E99.E7C86 2011
  979.8004'9712—dc22   2010049080

All rights reserved. Published in 2011 by Children's Press, an imprint of Scholastic Inc.
Printed in China 62
SCHOLASTIC, CHILDREN'S PRESS, A TRUE BOOK and associated logos are trademarks and/or registered trademarks of Scholastic Inc.

1 2 3 4 5 6 7 8 9 10 R 19 18 17 16 15 14 13 12 11

Find the Truth!

Everything you are about to read is true *except* for one of the sentences on this page.

Which one is **TRUE**?

T or F The Inuit eat raw meat.

T or F The Inuit have exactly five different words for snow.

Find the answers in this book.

Contents

THE **BIG** TRUTH!

The Amazing Caribou

Carved walrus tusk

Wood carving

3 Travel by Land and Sea

4 Inuit Society

Inuit coats called amauts have pockets for carrying babies.

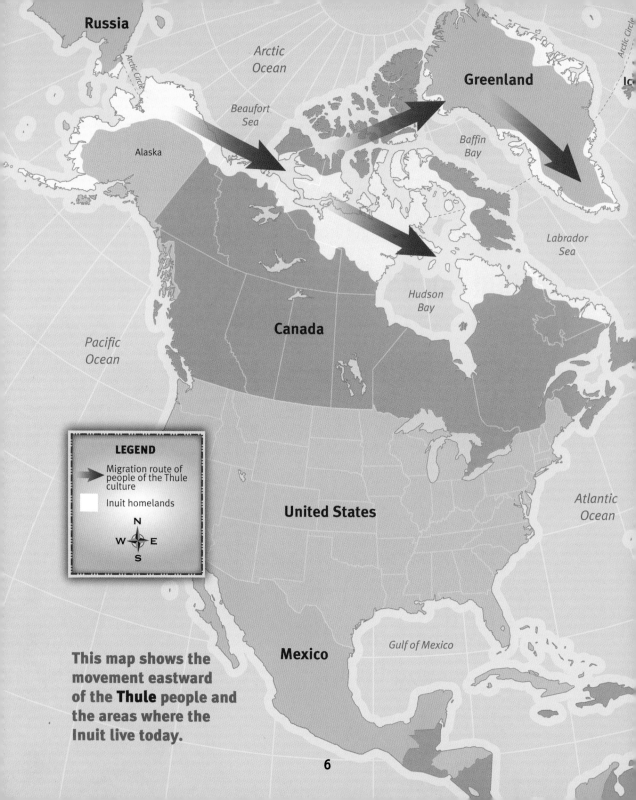

Russia

Arctic
Ocean

Greenland

Beaufort
Sea

Baffin
Bay

Alaska

Labrador
Sea

Hudson
Bay

Pacific
Ocean

Canada

LEGEND

Migration route of
people of the Thule
culture

Inuit homelands

N
W   E
S

United States

Atlantic
Ocean

Mexico

Gulf of Mexico

**This map shows the
movement eastward
of the Thule people and
the areas where the
Inuit live today.**

CHAPTER 1

Early Inuit History

The Inuit have always been an Arctic people. The cold, **tundra**, and icy seas influence everything in their lives. Today, the Inuit live in eastern Siberia, across northern Alaska and Canada, and in Greenland. But 1,100 years ago, the Inuit's ancestors, the people of the Thule culture, made their home on the Alaskan coast.

An individual member of the Inuit people is called an Inuk.

People of the Thule culture made the framework of houses from whalebones.

The Thule Culture

People in the Thule culture built houses with stone floors. Whalebone walls were covered with rock, animal skins, and a layer of sod. They lived in small groups of fewer than 50 people. When traveling on land, they used sleds made of driftwood and pulled by dogs. For sea travel, they built large boats called umiaks by tying walrus and seal skins over a driftwood frame.

Around the year 1000 C.E., members of the Thule culture began moving east. Along the way they encountered a people they called the Tuniit. The Tuniit belonged to the simpler Dorset culture. They lacked dogs for drawing sleds and bows and arrows for bringing down food such as **caribou** and polar bears. By the 1200s, the Thule peoples had better tools and weapons. This allowed them to drive away the Tuniit and settle in western Greenland.

The Inuit carve pictures on walrus tusks.

Inuits sometimes carve the story of hunts or other events on treasured objects.

Once in Greenland, the Thule peoples encountered travelers from across the Atlantic Ocean—the Vikings. The Vikings called the native peoples they met Skraelings. At times, the two groups may have traded. Viking writings state that at other times they fought. How often it happened is unknown. Both the Thule peoples and the Vikings hunted during the summer on Greenland's eastern coast. This is probably where they encountered one another.

Inuit people in Greenland

The Algonquin gave the Inuit the name Eskimos.

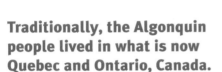

Traditionally, the Algonquin people lived in what is now Quebec and Ontario, Canada.

In Canada, meanwhile, a shift in climate that experts call the Little Ice Age made the Arctic colder. The Thule peoples moved farther south. No longer could they hunt the whales they had once used for meat, homes, and umiaks. As the Thule traveled, they encountered other Native American peoples such as the Algonquin. The two groups did not get along very well. Over time and with their travels, the ways of the Thule changed. They eventually developed into a new people known as the Inuit.

The Arctic is both
cold and very dry.
It is actually
a desert.

CHAPTER 2

Survival in the Arctic

To live in the Arctic's extreme cold demands toughness. To get by, human beings need high-energy food, special clothing, and the right tools. Their homes have to protect against frigid temperatures and howling winds. The Thule peoples and later the Inuit and other Arctic peoples, such as the Aleut and the Yupik, became experts in meeting the challenges. Arctic life, however, has never been easy. Even today, with electricity, packaged food, and snowmobiles, Arctic life is not easy for most people.

The Search for Food

The tundra ground thaws only a few inches deep in summer and only for a short time. Because of the lack of good soil, as well as the Arctic's short warm season, the Inuit were unable to grow crops. Instead, they survived by hunting, fishing, and gathering plant foods such as berries, roots, and seaweed. For most Inuit, meat from wild animals was the most important source of food.

Inuits used **harpoons** to hunt seals and walruses.

> Fatty, protein-rich seal meat gave people strength and energy.

Ringed seals weigh up to 150 pounds (70 kilograms).

A Seal Meal

Seal sometimes made up half of the Inuit diet. Inuit went after all kinds of seals and hunted in the same way as polar bears. Bears wait by holes that seals make in the ice in order to surface and breathe. Like the bears, an Inuit hunter lay on the ice next to an airhole with his harpoon, a spear with a sharp tip made of bone.

The hunter would drop a wood chip or other "floater" into the water. Just before the seal appeared, the floater moved. This let the hunter know the seal was coming. He timed his harpoon thrust for when the seal came up through the hole. Then he dragged the seal onto the ice. When finished, he made a **sacrifice** to Sedna, the water spirit. This showed respect for the seal's spirit. Not doing so brought bad luck, the Inuit believed. Inuit often ate the meat raw where they had made the kill.

A hunter waits for a seal to appear.

Hunters scratch the ice with seal claws to attract seals.

The Inuit people depended on food from the sea.

The Mighty Bowhead

Inuit gathered into groups to hunt large animals such as walruses, narwhals, and especially the 65-foot (20-meter) bowhead whale. When whaling, 20 hunters set out in an umiak and launched a harpoon dragging air-filled seal skin bags. The bags kept a bowhead from plunging into deep water after it was hit. Then, whenever it surfaced for air, the hunters harpooned it again. They continued to attack the whale until it died.

In Europe, the caribou is called the reindeer.

Caribou can swim 6 miles per hour (10 kilometers per hour).

Other Meat

Groups of Inuit also hunted the huge, dangerous walrus. When not hunting, men and sometimes women fished for Arctic cod and lake trout. They usually ate the fish raw. Groups of hunters also tracked the large herds of caribou over the tundra. In addition to spearing the animals, hunters tried to drive caribou into rivers. This made the caribou easier to catch.

Long-Lived Giants

The bowhead whale may have the longest life span of any animal. This was proven in 2007, when a 130-year-old harpoon tip was dug out of a bowhead that had recently been killed in Alaska. The tip dated to about 1880, meaning the whale had been alive in that year. Scientists believe the bowhead was even older. Because native hunters never killed calves, the whale must have been at least a few years old when it was harpooned.

Inuits traditionally dressed in furs to keep warm.

Clothing

Animals provided the Inuit with clothes as well as food. Inuit women turned animal skins into shirts, leggings (pants), shoes, and boots. They used bone needles and made thread from **tendon**. For an Inuit hunter, a woman's skill with needle and thread meant the difference between life and death. Men depended on their clothes to stay warm and dry. A flaw in a boot, for example, could lead to frostbite and death.

Knowing Your Sewing

Women found the strongest, best tendon in the back of the caribou. In addition, the caribou's skin made excellent clothing. The animal's hollow hairs trapped air. As a result, clothing made from caribou hide was both warm and lightweight. To make clothes, the women sewed a double line of tiny stitches together tightly. Water caused the tendon thread to get bigger. When it did, it filled the hole created by the needle.

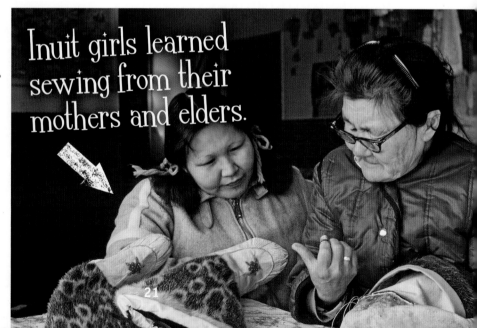

Inuits make boots from seal or caribou skin.

Inuit girls learned sewing from their mothers and elders.

21

The Anorak

For the Inuit, no clothing item was more important than the **anorak**, or parka. These coats were made from caribou or seal skin or sometimes from the intestine of a seal. The anorak had to resist windchills of –100 degrees Fahrenheit (–73 degrees Celsius). They also kept the wearer dry during boat journeys and whale hunts. Some anoraks looked like modern raincoats. Others were lined with fur from the polar bear, fox, or wolverine.

Women wore hoods that could cover a baby on her back.

Kamik (or mukluks) were soft boots made of skin. They were often lined with fox or rabbit fur. The Inuit also carved snow goggles from horn or antlers. These cut the blinding glare of the sunlight as it bounced off the white snow and ice. The Inuit rubbed the inside of the goggles with dark soot for added protection. From head to toe, the Inuit depended on animals, and their own skill, to supply what was needed for survival.

Snow goggles let through only a small amount of light.

The Amazing Caribou

Every summer, caribou gather into gigantic herds and walk hundreds of miles toward feeding grounds. Once there, a caribou may eat 12 pounds (5 kg) of grass and other plants per day. A large male can stand 5 feet (1.5 m) high—taller if you include the antlers—and weigh 350 to 400 pounds (160 to 180 kg) on average. Caribou are famous for their role in Inuit life. But the animal itself is extraordinary.

Temperature Control

The unusual arteries and veins in a caribou's legs allow the temperature in the legs to drop to 50°F (10°C) without harming the animal. The body temperature elsewhere remains normal.

Female Antlers

Female caribou are the only female deer to grow antlers. They use them to fight off wolves while guarding their calves.

Fat Antifreeze

Caribou fat remains a liquid in low temperatures. The unusual fat helps the caribou survive the freezing Arctic winter.

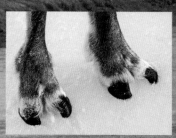

A skilled builder could put up an iglu in an hour.

House of Snow

The Inuit word ***iglu*** (IG-loo) means house. Inuit used the word for any dwelling. The famous snow house that English speakers call the igloo was only used by Inuit in Greenland and parts of Canada. To make an iglu, the builder used a knife made from bone or horn to cut blocks of snow from a *piqsiq,* or snowdrift. Cutting blocks left a pit in the snow. The builder then used the blocks to build a dome over the pit.

The sleeping area in the pit lay below the snow level outside the iglu. The Inuit polished the blocks to make them fit together. A well-made iglu was strong enough to support a person standing on the roof. It was also warm. The snow piled outside plus the air trapped in the snow blocks acted as **insulation**. As a result, the inside of an iglu was sometimes heated up to 60°F (15.5°C).

An Inuit man opens the door on his iglu.

Light and Heat

An Inuit family could make the iglu warmer by lighting a **kudlik**, a lamp of carved soapstone filled with seal or whale oil. The lamp provided not only light but heat. A family used its kudlik to cook, dry clothes, and melt snow for drinking water. The Inuit called snow melted for water *aniuk* (ah-nee-OOK). In fact, the Inuit had more than 30 different words for snow.

An Inuit woman tends her kudlik.

Seal and whale oil came from the fat of each animal.

28

The Inuit sometimes built homes out of rocks, sod, and whalebone.

In some parts of the Arctic, the Inuit might spend the summer months in tents. Like their Thule ancestors, these Inuit stretched seal or caribou skins over a frame made of wood or whalebones. In Alaska, the Inuit preferred houses built of stone and frozen sod. Other Inuit built small structures out of driftwood. Twenty people might live in a large house. People hung up skins to create walls.

Huskies can withstand
temperatures as cold as
−75°F (−60°C).

CHAPTER 3

Travel by Land and Sea

The Inuit used several clever inventions to travel the rough Arctic landscape. On land, the dogsled was the main way of getting around. The Inuit made the sled from wood or animal bones and set it on runners that glided across snow. A dogsled carried goods and an Inuit musher (driver), who steered. A team of dogs, the ancestors of today's huskies and malamutes, pulled the load.

 Inuit called a dogsled a qamutik (caw-MOO-tick).

Art and Spirit

Inuit art is famous around the world. Members of both the Dorset and Thule cultures carved animal shapes and masks out of bone, caribou antler, walrus tusk, and stone. The Inuit who shaped the figurines and other items believed their works had the power to keep away evil or allow them to contact spirits. Members of the Thule peoples also made everyday items that ranged from buttons and earrings to harpoons.

Comb in the shape of a woman

Making the Journey

An Inuit musher used landmarks such as rivers and hills to guide him on his journey. The tundra, however, was often a flat plain where everything looked the same. In that case, the musher built a pile of stones called an **inuksuk**. This served as a sign pointing a traveler in the right direction. An inuksuk had other uses. It could show a good hunting spot, mark a food storage location, or fence in caribou to be killed.

The 2010 Winter Olympics logo was based on an inuksuk.

Some inuksuks have a human shape.

Kayaks were sometimes 20 feet (6 m) long.

The Inuit invented kayaks.

On the Water

Inuit living on the coast used different kinds of boats for different jobs. The one-man kayak was covered in waterproof seal skin and built especially to fit its owner's body. Thanks to its shape, the kayak was almost impossible to tip over. Even when it did, the kayaker could easily roll the boat back into position. The Inuit built a faster type of long kayak to travel great distances.

The Inuit used the larger umiak to carry dogs, goods, and larger numbers of people. To build an umiak, the Inuit fitted together pieces of driftwood with pegs and tied cords. Seal skin was then stretched over the frame. A large umiak might be 30 feet (9 m) long. Inuit sailors could bring the flat-bottomed boat close to shore. That made the umiak an excellent boat for hauling goods from one hunting ground to the next.

About seven seal skins are needed to cover one large umiak.

An Inuit couple

CHAPTER 4

Inuit Society

Inuit men and women each had clear roles. The men hunted and fished. Women cooked, sewed, and raised the children, though some women also fished. Because men spent long periods away on hunts, women had to be strong and independent. At the same time, men had to know how to cook and sew for themselves when away from home.

Most Inuit got married. Families, in fact, sometimes arranged a marriage years before their children became adults.

The Inuit did not have wedding ceremonies.

Marriage

Inuit marriages often included more than one wife or husband. If a man was leaving on a journey, for example, he might trade his sick wife to another man for a healthier wife who could manage the home. Survival depended on man-woman teamwork. If children were born from such marriages, they considered it normal to have two mothers and two fathers.

Timeline of Inuit History

1000 C.E.
Inuit ancestors known as Thule move east from the Alaskan coast.

1200
The Thule meet Vikings.

A Large Family at Home

An Inuit family often included more people than just a father, mother, and children. The children's grandparents might live with the family. In some cases, uncles and aunts and their children lived with them, too. But every household had one head. This man was respected for his wisdom and experience. Though Inuit men and women considered themselves equals in many ways, the men made the important decisions.

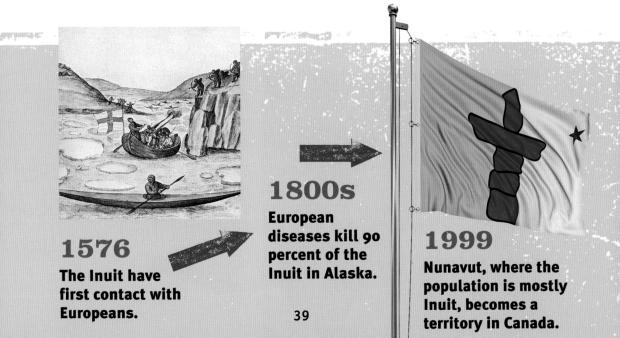

1576
The Inuit have first contact with Europeans.

1800s
European diseases kill 90 percent of the Inuit in Alaska.

1999
Nunavut, where the population is mostly Inuit, becomes a territory in Canada.

Taboos

Inuit society did not have government or laws. But people understood the difference between right and wrong actions. Inuit considered some actions **taboo** and never did them. For example, it was taboo to murder an Inuit elder. An elder taught important lessons about survival skills and the Inuit religion. Killing him robbed all Inuit of the elder's valuable knowledge. If an Inuit broke such a taboo, the community called in a **shaman** to make things right.

Inuits learn from their elders.

Some Inuits believed that breaking a taboo brought bad weather.

Inuits traveled to trading posts to exchange furs for other goods.

European explorers and traders had contact with the Inuit first in Greenland in 1576 and later in Canada and Alaska. After contact, however, the Inuit began dying in great numbers from European diseases. In western Alaska, for example, 90 percent of the Inuit died in the 1800s. The Inuit had no idea that germs were to blame. Instead, they believed they had angered the animal spirits by not properly sacrificing to the gods before eating their food.

Changing Ways

Today, differences between the Inuit and Europeans still affect Inuit society. The Inuit continue to adjust to new ways. Their challenge is to find ways to honor the traditions of their elders while living in today's rapidly changing world. ★

In Canada's Nunavut Territory, 83 percent of the people are Inuit.

Girls from Nunavut dressed in traditional clothing

Amount of calories Inuit got from fat: 75 percent

Weight of a large caribou: 400 to 700 lbs. (180 to 320 kg)

Length of large bowhead whale: 65 ft. (20 m)

Number of hunters in a large umiak: 20

Temperature inside an iglu: 60°F (16°C)

Number of Inuit words for snow: More than 30

Length of the largest kayaks: 20 ft. (6 m)

Depth of a kayak: About 7 in. (18 cm)

Length of a large umiak: 30 ft. (9 m)

Percentage of Greenlanders with Inuit blood: 90 percent

Percentage of western Inuit who died in 1800s: 90 percent

Number of people in Nunavut: 32,900

Did you find the truth?

(T) The Inuit eat raw meat.

(F) The Inuit have exactly five different words for snow.

Resources

Books

Alexander, Cherry. *Inuit*. New York: PowerKids, 2009.

Haskins, Lori. *Sled Dogs*. New York: Bearport, 2006.

Ipellie, Altootook, and David MacDonald. *The Inuit Thought of It*. Toronto: Annick Press, 2007.

King, David C. *The Inuit*. New York: Benchmark, 2007.

Steltzer, Ulli. *Building an Igloo*. New York: Henry Holt, 1999.

Wallace, Mary. *The Inuksuk Book*. Toronto: Maple Tree, 2004.

Williams, Suzanne M. *The Inuit*. New York: Children's Press, 2004.

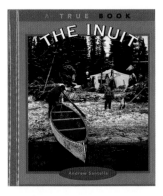

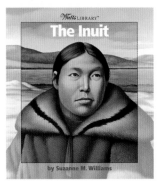

Organizations and Web Sites

Inuit Culture and Legends—Scholastic.com

http://www2.scholastic.com/browse/article.jsp?id=4612

Learn about the stories and songs Inuit use to entertain each other.

Museum of Inuit Art

www.miamuseum.ca

Study Inuit sculpture and carvings from Canada's largest Inuit art museum.

PBS Nature—The Living Edens: Arctic Oasis

www.pbs.org/wnet/nature/arcticoasis/index.html

Read about an Inuit boy growing up in northern Canada and the film that followed his life.

Places to Visit

Anchorage Museum

625 C Street
Anchorage, AK 99501
(907) 929-9200
www.anchoragemuseum.org/index.aspx
See art and other items created by Alaska's Inuit people.

Canadian Museum of Civilization

100 Laurier Street
Gatineau, Quebec K1A 0M8
(800) 555-5621
www.civilization.ca/splash.html
Visit exhibits on Canada's history and place of the Inuit in it.

Important Words

anorak (AN-or-ak) — a hooded coat with a seal skin outer shell

caribou (KA-ri-boo) — reindeer

harpoons (har-POONZ) — long spears used to hunt seal and whale

iglu (IG-loo) — Inuit homes made from blocks of snow

insulation (in-suh-LAY-shuhn) — any material used to keep a house warm

inuksuk (in-UK-shook or in-UK-suk) — piled rocks used as a marker for travelers

kamik (KAH-mik) — soft, fur-lined waterproof boots

kudlik (KUH-dlik) — a soapstone lamp in which seal or whale oil is burned

sacrifice (SAK-ruh-fisse) — something valuable given to a god or spirit

shaman (SHAH-mun or SHAY-mun) — a holy man and healer

taboo (tuh-BU or TA-boo) — something prohibited

tendon (TEN-duhn) — stringy tissue that attaches muscle to bone

Thule (THU-lee or THYU) — the early Inuit people

tundra (TUHN-druh) — flat, treeless plain found in the Arctic

Index

Page numbers in **bold** indicate illustrations

About the Authors

Kevin Cunningham has written more than 40 books on disasters, the history of disease, Native Americans, and other topics. Cunningham lives near Chicago with his wife and young daughter.

Peter Benoit is educated as a mathematician but has many other interests. He has taught and tutored high school and college students for many years, mostly in math and science. He also runs summer workshops for writers and students of literature. Benoit has written more than 2,000 poems. His life has been one committed to learning. He lives in Greenwich, New York.